Meet the Horses
Mustang Horses

by Rachel Grack

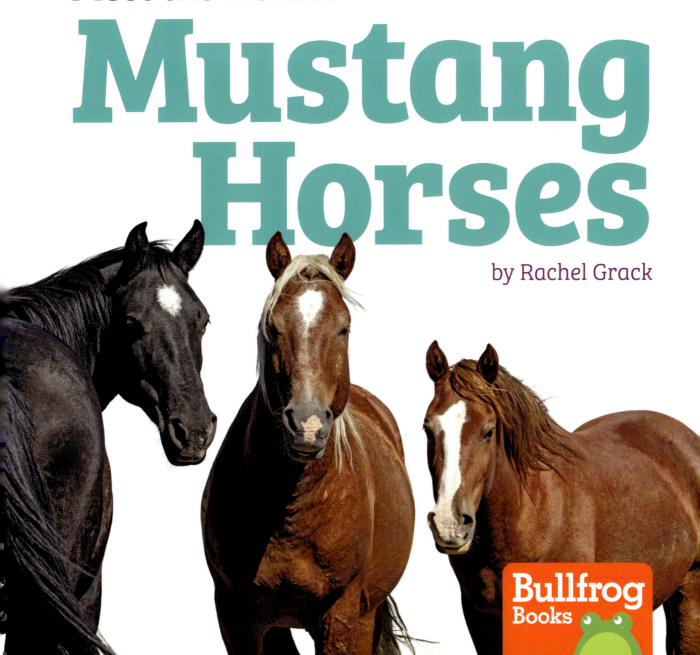

Ideas for Parents and Teachers

Bullfrog Books let children practice reading informational text at the earliest reading levels. Repetition, familiar words, and photo labels support early readers.

Before Reading
- Discuss the cover photo. What does it tell them?
- Look at the picture glossary together. Read and discuss the words.

During Reading
- "Walk" through the book with the reader. Discuss new or unfamiliar words. Sound them out together.
- Look at the photos together. Point out the photo labels.

After Reading
- Prompt the child to think more. Ask: Have you ever seen a mustang? Where was it?

Bullfrog Books are published by Jump!
5357 Penn Avenue South
Minneapolis, MN 55419
www.jumplibrary.com

Copyright © 2026 Jump! International copyright reserved in all countries. No part of this book may be reproduced in any form without written permission from the publisher.

Jump! is a division of FlutterBee Education Group.

Library of Congress Cataloging-in-Publication Data

Names: Koestler-Grack, Rachel A., 1973– author
Title: Mustang horses / by Rachel Grack.
Description: Minneapolis, MN: Jump!, Inc., [2026]
Series: Meet the horses | Includes index.
Audience: Ages 5–8
Identifiers: LCCN 2024048470 (print)
LCCN 2024048471 (ebook)
ISBN 9798892139489 (hardcover)
ISBN 9798892139496 (paperback)
ISBN 9798892139502 (ebook)
Subjects: LCSH: Mustang—Juvenile literature
Classification: LCC SF293.M9 K636 2026 (print)
LCC SF293.M9 (ebook)
DDC 599.665/5—dc23/eng/20241227
LC record available at https://lccn.loc.gov/2024048470
LC ebook record available at https://lccn.loc.gov/2024048471

Editor: Katie Chanez
Designer: Molly Ballanger
Content Consultant: Becky Robb Hotzler; Wells Creek Wild Mustang Sanctuary; This Old Horse, Inc.

Photo Credits: mariait/Shutterstock, cover; Tom Tietz/Shutterstock, 1, 14–15, 23tr; twildlife/iStock, 3, 16, 18–19, 23tm; Chris Sattlberger/Blend Images/SuperStock, 4; Rob Palmer Photography/Shutterstock, 5, 23br; Wildphotos/Dreamstime, 6–7, 23bm; Lynn Bell Thompson/Shutterstock, 8–9, 23tl; John Morrison/iStock, 10, 24; Drazen_/iStock, 11; htrnr/iStock, 12–13, 23bl; Jorn Vangoidtsenhoven/Dreamstime, 17; Taiga/Shutterstock, 20–21; yenwen/iStock, 22.

Printed in the United States of America at Corporate Graphics in North Mankato, Minnesota.

Table of Contents

Wild and Free	4
A Look at a Mustang Horse	22
Picture Glossary	23
Index	24
To Learn More	24

Wild and Free

Wild horses run.

They are mustangs.

prairie

They live on **prairies**.

Some have brown **coats**. Others are white or black.

They have strong legs.

They run fast.

They have hard **hooves**.
They walk on rocks.

hoof

Many live in **herds**.

They eat grass.

They find water to drink.

Foals play.

Moms stay close.

They grow up.

They stay with the herd!

A Look at a Mustang Horse

What are the parts of a mustang horse? Take a look!

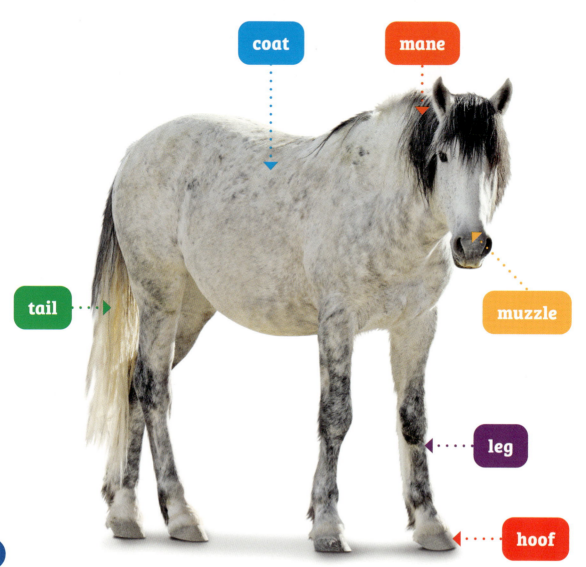

Picture Glossary

coats
Hair on horses.

foals
Young horses.

herds
Groups of horses.

hooves
The hard parts that cover a horse's feet.

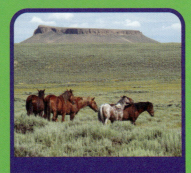

prairies
Large areas of flat grassland with few or no trees.

wild
Living in natural conditions and not cared for by humans.

Index

coats 8
drink 17
eat 16
fast 11
foals 18
herds 15, 21

hooves 12
legs 10
prairies 7
run 4, 11
strong 10
wild 4

To Learn More

Finding more information is as easy as 1, 2, 3.
❶ Go to **www.factsurfer.com**
❷ Enter **"mustanghorses"** into the search box.
❸ Choose your book to see a list of websites.